BE SEATED, THOU

We may return to Mozart.
He was young, and we, we are old.
The snow is falling
And the streets are full of cries.
Be seated, thou.

— Wallace Stevens ("Mozart", 1935)

Be Seated, Thou

Poems 1989-1998

Dannie Abse

THE SHEEP MEADOW PRESS
RIVERDALE-ON-HUDSON, NEW YORK

All inquiries and permission requests should be addressed to:
The Sheep Meadow Press
PO Box 1345
Riverdale-on-Hudson, NY 10471

Designed and typeset by S.M.

Printed on acid-free paper in the United States. This book meets the guidelines for permanence and durability of the Committee on Production Guidelines for Book Longevity of the Council on Library Resources.

The Library of Congress Cataloging-in-Publication Data

Abse, Dannie.
    Be seated, thou: poems / Dannie Abse.
        p. cm.
    ISBN 1-878818-83-X (acid-free paper)

PR6001.B7 B4 1999
821'.914--dc21

                                                    99-045750

Acknowledgements

Acknowledgements are owed to the BBC for new poems broadcast, including those of the 1996 Edinburgh Festival's Stanza on Stage.

Some poems were first published in the following English and Welsh periodicals and books: *Acumen, Aquarius, The Author, The Jewish Chronicle, The Jewish Quarterly, The Lancet, London Magazine, The New Statesman, The New Welsh Review, New Writing* (British Council), *The Observer, Planet, P N Review, The Poetry Book Society Anthology, The Poetry Review, The Poet's View, Poetry Wales, Stand, The Spectator, The Sunday Times,* and *Welsh Retrospective* (Seren).

Others appeared in: *The Georgia Review, The Iowa Review, Michigan Quarterly Review, Pivot, Ploughshares, Poetry, TriQuarterly,* and *Quarterly Review of Literature.*

Table of Contents

On the Evening Road

Proposal

Herschel, thrilled, observed a new star
and named it to honour a King;

Dr. Livingstone found for his Queen
a waterfall 'smoke which sounded';

and tactful Corot gave Daumier
a house 'to upset the landlord'.

What dare I promise? Mountain signposts
are few and treasures I have none.

Yet come with me, congenial, far,
up the higher indigo roads.

There, memory is imagination
and we may find an eagle's feather.

The Green Field

As soft-eyed lovers for the very first time,
turning out the light for the first time,
blot out all detail, all colours,
and whisper the old code-words, 'Love you',

so those admiring that patch of grass,
there, on the hillside, from this distance
could be in the dark, unconcerned with detail.
'That green field,' they generalize,

though drawing nearer (as to a poem)
they will discover the lies of distance:
rage of different greens. And at the field itself
an unforeseen tapestry of variousness:

sprawl of common weeds and wild flowers,
subtleties of small petals seldom green.

Talking to Blake

I saw a lit candle in sunlight
held by the ghost of William Blake.
He walked by the polluted river, ill-at-ease,
beneath Lambeth's dusty poplar trees.

Then high above Parliament Big Ben struck
and his voice advised as from afar,
'Write visionary lines that give a moral light,
let a poem become a star.'

'Mr. Blake,' I replied, 'most poets make
a pale sound now—like a falling snowflake
and the roar of machinery grows
with the automation of the rose.

Deafened, deafened, are the beautiful Nine
so what you once said remains as true,
the languid strings do scarcely move,
the sound is forc'd, the notes are few.

All our permutations of despair,
smouldering word-fires without light or heat,
our pursuance of the incomplete,
leave no disturbance in the air.'

'Then,' said he, lowering the candlestick,
(as if to examine a grain of sand)
'the Rose of English Poetry is sick
like England's green and pleasant land.'

Condensation on a Windowpane

1

I want to write something simple,
something simple, few adjectives,
ambiguities disallowed.

Something old-fashioned:
a story of Time perhaps
or, more daringly, of love.

I want to write something simple
that everyone can understand,
something simple as pure water.

But pure water
is H_2O
and that's complicated
like steam, like ice, like clouds.

2

My finger squeaks on glass.
I write JOAN
I write DANNIE.
Imagine! I'm a love-struck
youth again.

I want to say something
without ambiguity.
Imagine! Me, old-age pensioner
wants to say something
to do with love and Time,
love that's simple as water.

But long ago we learnt
water is complicated,
is H_2O, is ice, is steam, is cloud.

Our names on the window
begin to fade.
Slowly, slowly.
They weep as they vanish.

How I won the Raffle

After I won the raffle with the number 1079,
the Master of Ceremonies asked me why.
'Why did you select that particular number?'

'A man's character is his fate,' I replied,
leaning lazily on a quote as usual.

And suddenly I thought of Schopenhauer's
two last men in the world, two gaunt hermits,
meeting each other in the wilderness,

how an amiable man like Pufendorf
might postulate they'd shake hands;
a Hobbes they'd kill each other;
a Rousseau they'd pass each other by
in terrible silence.

'In short,' said the Master of Ceremonies impatiently,
'you chose 1079 because you had to.'

'In short, I chose 10 because in the old days
ten men used to dance around a new grave.

I chose 7 because those ten men used to dance
around the new grave seven times.'

Also because of the pyramids of Egypt;
the hanging gardens of Babylon;
Diana's Temple at Ephesus;
the great statue of Zeus at Athens;
the Mausoleum at Halicarnassus;
the Colossus of Rhodes;
and the lighthouse of Alexandria.

'I chose 9 because among all numbers
it looks most like a musical note;
nine because of the nine orders of Angels;
nine because of the nine rivers of Hell.'

Also because of Clio with her backward look;
Calliope, stern, staring at her scroll;
Erato, nude, except for her brassière;
Euterpe, eyes closed, flute in mouth;
Terpsichore dancing away, silly one;
Melpomene, arms raised, dagger in hand;
Thalia, mirthless, behind her laughing mask;
Polyhymnia, in sacred robes, orating;
and Urania, dreamy, head amid the stars.

'Sir,' I said,
to the scowling Master of Ceremonies,
'that's why I chose the winning number
1079.'

Between 3 and 4 a.m.

1

Wakeful at 3 a.m.
near the frontiers of Nothing
it's easy, so easy
to imagine (like William Blake)
an archaic angel standing
in a cone of light
not of this world;

easy at the cheating hour
to believe an angel cometh
to touch babies' skulls,
their fontanelles,
deleting the long memory
of generations —
(only prodigies not visited);

easy to conceive angel-light
bright as that sudden,
ordinary window
I saw at midnight
across the road
before the drawing
of its blind.

2

Once, another presence
also nocturnal, oneiric,
secretive, in disguise,
waiting behind
an opening Seder door.

'No,' says the child. 'Gone.'
Framed in that black oblong,
nobody.

(A shadow flies
when a light is shone.)

Was childhood real?
Did a stallion attempt
to mount a mare
painted by Apelles?
Did Greek workmen hear
the exiled statue sob
when carried to
Lord Elgin's ship?

The mystery named
is not the mystery caged.

Even a night-scene
may be an illusion
like an afternoon harbour
viewed through sunglasses,
the light forged
to a moon-tortured sea.

3

I was visited once, once only, elsewhere,
near a lake, near an oak,
near a weeping willow tree and thorn
one summertime, out of time, in England,
during the cosmic love-making hour
when day and night shyly intermingled,

when day, entranced, did not know what or who
and night, ecstatic, was not itself entirely
till the slow coming of the stars.
But now, weeping willow tree and thorn,
there's only the dread of Nothing.

(Nothing, say the kabbalists
is more real than nothing.)

It's 4 a.m. already and cold
and quiet, quiet as a long
abandoned battlefield.

Late to trawl, net full of holes,
the grounded darkness
for what, naturally, can never be told.

(The unutterable, at best, becomes music.)

No, it's time to hold the silence found
on one side
with the right hand,
the silence on the other
with the left,
then to pull, pull, pull,

till silence tears without a sound.

The Mistake

Come this way through the wooden gate into our garden.
Confront the green tree which once had no identity.
Pluck a leaf. Close your eyes. Smell its acrid odour.
Does it suggest an Oriental dispensary?

One day (after thirteen years) a tree-expert told us
its name: '*Evodia danieli*, without doubt.
From Korea. Odd to find it thriving here in Wales.'
We thanked him. Now we had something to boast about.

When visitors came we offered them a leaf proudly.
'Breathe this in,' we'd urge. 'It's rare as Welsh gold.'
Our olfactory gift, our pagan benediction.
'From Korea,' we'd swank. 'It'll charm away your cold.'

Who, in all of Great Britain, possessed such treasure?
But then came the summer of the drought. Tired of lies
the parched tree suddenly asserted itself, sprouted
ordinary walnuts, shamelessly free of disguise.

A Doctor's Register

And yet God has not said a word!
                    Porphyria's Lover, *R. Browning*

Half asleep, you recalled a fading list
of girls' sweet names. Now to old women
these names belong — some whom you tumbled and kissed
in summer's twilit lanes or hidden by heather.
You were a youth who never stayed long
for Gwen or for Joyce, for Rita or Ruth
and there were others too, on a lower register.

Then, suddenly, a robust, scolding voice
changed your dream's direction and the weather:
'That much morphia, doctor? Wrong, wrong.'

Surprised to discover your eyes still shut
you wondered which dead patient or what
(whose accusing son and when?) as any
trusted doctor would who did not murder
any pleading one with sovereign impunity.

'I found a thing to do,' said the lover
of Porphyria. *Porphyria?* Awake you add
the other pretty names too: Anuria,
Filaria, Leukaemia, Melanoma,
Sarcoma, Euthanasia, amen.

The Excavation

Absurd those tall stories of tall heroes.
Mine, too. Sixty ells, they said, between
my shoulders! Happy legends of my strength!
Hippy myths of my hair! How I lifted up
a mountain here, a mountain there. Dig, dig:
so little recorded, so many exaggerations.

Three hundred foxes, they said, remember?
Nine, only nine. With a jawbone of an ass,
they said, I topped a thousand men. Dig, dig
for their gritty skulls. I unthatched a mere ten.
Let others boast that I was 'magic',
the rainbow spirit of the Lord about me.

But absent, He, when the whips cracked and I
was led, eyeless, into Dagon's Temple,
heard the hooting crazies on the roof. So many,
the junk Temple collapsed thunderously.
Joke! They thought *I'd* brought the House down —
me, clapped-out circus act, defunct Strong Man.

I was screaming, believe me, I was lost.
Betrayed, betrayed, and so little recorded:
the brevities of a Hebrew scribe only;
a fable for a Milton to embroider;
a picture for a Rubens to paint;
music for the soul of a Saint-Saëns.

Dig, dig, though you will not find Dagon's stone
fish-tail nor the scissors of the sung star
of the Philistines. Who knows the path of that whore
after the Temple, unglued, crashed and crushed?
Did she return to Sorek or raise once more
her aprons in the brothels of Philistia?

Dig, dig. I hear your questing spades muffled,
south of Gaza. Useless. The shifting sands
have buried deeper the graves of all.
Only the wilderness remains, silence
and a jawbone. And marvellous ghosts
people a yellow page of Judges.

History

(To Peter Vansittart)

The last war-horse slaughtered and eaten
long ago. Not a rat, not a crow-crumb
left; the polluted water scarce;
the vile flies settling on the famous
enlarged eyes of skeleton children.

Tonight the moon's open-mouthed. I must
surrender in the morning. But those
cipher tribes out there, those Golden Hordes,
those shit! They'll loot and maim and rape.
What textbook atrocities in the morning?

Now, solitary, my hip-joint aching,
half-lame, I climb the high battlements
carrying a musical instrument.
Why not? What's better? The bedlam of sleep
or the clarities of insomnia?

Look! Below, most fearful perspective:
cloud-fleeing shadows of unending
flatlands; enemy tent after tent
pegged to the unstable moonlight.
You'd think the moon, exposed, would howl.

Besieged city, in some future
history book (aseptic page or footnote)
they'll fable your finale: how
your huck-shouldered, arthritic General,
silhouette on the dark battlements,

played on his pipe a Mongolian song,
an enemy song, played so purely
the Past disrobed, memory made audible,
(sharp as a blade, lonely, most consequent,
that soul-naked melody of the steppes);

how, below, the Mongol soldiers awoke,
listened, leaned on their elbows tamed,
became so utterly homesick, wretched,
so inflamed, that by the cold sweats
of dawnlight, they decamped, departed.

Ha! Such a pleasing, shameless story,
to be told over and over by these
and by those: by propagandists of music;
by descendants of the Mongols.
But, alas, only a scribe's invention.

The truth? I play pianissimo
and not very well. The sleepers
in their tents sleep on, the sentries
hardly stir. I loiter on the battlements.
Stars! Stars! I put away my pipe and weep.

Meurig Dafydd to his Mistress

No word I huffed when Stradling urged the squire
to throw my eulogy on the fire.
The fiddlers laughed. I, snow-silent, proud,
did not melt. But I'm spitless now,
my pearl, my buttercup, my bread-fruit.
I rattle their silver in my pocket.
I have other stanzas for harp and lute,
other gullible lords to flatter.
What do I care for that big-bellied Englishman,
that bugle, that small-beer, that puff-ball,
that dung-odoured sonneteer, John Stradling?

Does he sing perfect meter like Taliesin?
Not that gout-toed, goat-faced manikin.
What does he know of Welsh necks crayoned
by the axe, blood on our feet, our history?
Has he stood pensive at the tomb
of Morien, or Morial, or March?
Wept at any nervous harp, at the gloom
of a dirge for Llywelyn the Last,
or the lament by Lewis Glyn Cothi?
That fungoid, that bunt, that broken-wind,
that bog-bean, can't tell a song from a grunt.

Clean heart, my theology, my sweet-briar,
he'd put our heritage on the fire.
Each night he swigs mead in a safe bed —
never sleeps roofed only by the stars.
At noon, never signs the euphonious nine
sermons of the blackbird. O my lotus,
his lexicon is small compared to mine.

His verses are like standing urine — tepid.
My Welsh stanzas have more heat in them
than the tumbling flames in the fire-place
of the Minstrel Hall of Bewpyr.

Ya

The machine began to hum.
Some blood, they pleaded,
just a little, uncoagulated,
fresh blood, please.
It was springtime, springtime,
the season to open doors.
A pinprick? On the thumb?
They shook their heads.
Hesitant, scrupulous,
sullenly, we detached a finger
— under an anesthetic,
humanely, you understand.
But, afterwards, candid,
they demanded, More blood!
And, ya, after debate
we did amputate a hand:
soft tissues retracted,
joint opened cleanly,
lateral ligaments cut through.
From the wrist.
Better, they said hoarsely,
leaving us discomfited.
What else could we do?
Outside it was springtime, springtime,
the birds' hullabaloo;
the young cried as usual,
not knowing why,
the old because they knew.
So, ya, a whole arm,
almost a perfect job
and without an anesthetic too.
No wonder they applauded,
their obscene shouts, their keen whistles,

like hosannas from hell.
Allow us this though;
outside it was shifting sunlight,
it was wild bluebells
and, ya, one of us at the window
quoted an English poet-priest:
I do not think I've seen
anything more beautiful
than a bluebell.
I know the beauty
of our Lord by it.
So not till all the women
were released, banished,
did we consent to saw off
a raw foot. Right and left neatly,
our technique swift, improving.
And who could not respond
excitedly — that adrenal flow —
to their rhythmic chanting?
Ya, with both legs wide
then unhinged completely,
oh the powerful voltage
of their male applause
and oh the soulful thrilling
of our National Anthem.
So moving, so very moving,
man it was something.
Fellow scientists,
you can guess
what happened next,
ya, you know
the end of the story.

Beautiful Dead Poets

She spoke of Garcia Lorca murdered;
Hernandez dying in a Franco prison;
Mayakovsky's suicide; how Mandelstam
jumped through the window of a hospital;
Celan and Levi in the Nazi Death Camps.
'Beautiful dead poets, all of them,' said she,
in the delight of enthusiasm.

Behind her, a dark mahogany table
that once had the girth of a lofty tree;
a vase of deep red, drooping lovely things —
aged tulips — untimely ripped from the earth;
and, by the window, a canary caged
because it sang so beautifully.

Ghosting for Mayakovsky

(His suicide note)

1

It's long past one and you must be asleep.
The quiet night's astonished by all the stars.
Why wake you now with a telegram like thunder?

So many thoughts of mystery the night can bring.
So what? Our love boat's on the rocks. Its sails
wrenched from the mast. No use in adding up the cost,

we're quits; no need to weigh our hearts and hurts
upon the scales. 'No Life without you,' once I said,
and now the strokes of Two thud down like heads from blocks.

Our story's over, iconoclast. I'm lost. I'm through.
No need to wake you with a telegram like thunder.
Art's imperative will make these lines come true.

2

Once I drew the Queen of Hearts,
now I'm dealt another card. A club. A two.
Once forbidden love lit up like paper
then it charred.

Once with verse of lightning and half in song
I told a daisy and the world
you loved me, you love me not,
and how worthless life unfurled would be
without you — like a single shoe.
I'll not limp along.

I'm shot. I'm through.
Queen of Hearts, O Queen of Hearts,
the imperatives of Art insist,
the lies of Art come true.

Is Creation a Destructive Force?

1

Weary in the airport lounge
he read again the letters of Keats:
'I am with Achilles in the trenches,
with Theocritus in the vales of Sicily.'

Later, at the airport security,
crossing the doorless door,
an empty, revolver-like
click-terrorist, click-terrorist, click.

They searched him,
checked his identification papers,
found in his inside pocket
the pen that can annihilate self.

2

In the studio where she suddenly died,
on the easel still, Ingeborg's last canvas,
entrancing, unfinished, and of course unsigned.

Afflicted self-portrait. She crouches before
a half-open door — there's dark darkness behind
and, just visible, a stark foot's advancing.

Ludic Oblongs

First draw an oblong on an unlined page,
the shape of the page. Now what do you see?

No, Peter, no. Not an upright coffin.
Hardly, it's much too wide for a coffin.

A magician's box. Uh huh. Suppose so.
From which the blonde lady has disappeared

no doubt. What do you think, Melanie? Yes.
A window. Right. What do you see through it?

Snowfields? Acres of snowfields on and on?
Quiet, Mary. It's Melanie's window.

What? A frosted window? C'mon, hardly.
Someone in a bath behind it, perhaps?

Why are you laughing, Peter? What's that, Paul?
Mmm. A cage without bars. The bird has flown.

The bell rang then and I went home happy
till I thought of the real world and its ills.

Oh the uselessness of drawing oblongs
filled with trapped silence or white on white.

Still, here's another, here's its caption:
THE LOST WALK IN THE SAME DIRECTION

Breakfast Together

She sits opposite me
the other side of the breakfast table,
doesn't know that last week
I murdered her.

Oh pure, flawless love!
It would have altered — leaves are falling now —
with the passing years.

Consider the statistics of divorce.
The possible prolegomenon:
secret phone-calls,
furtive appointments,
marital violence even.

Man, man, never strike a woman
for if you do
she'll have dominion
over you.

No, no, not that. None of that
as the leaves fall, the passing years.

So I arranged her funeral,
no expense spared —
a secular funeral; a hush of black cars;
flowers galore, a veritable park!

The mortician's arms folded, head bowed.

I thought of playing that tape,
that Beethoven *Cavatina*,
that anguished music she loved best,
music so remote, so terrible.

Instead I chose the old dance-tune
my mother-in-law liked:
'Stay as sweet as you are,
don't let a thing ever change you.'
Appropriate, *n'est-ce-pas*?

Afterwards, the wake that I had planned.
A joyous feast! Drinks galore!
We had everything except balloons.

And there she is now, not knowing any of this,
sitting the other side of the table,
alluring still, spooning a grapefruit,
mirthless, reading the *Guardian* —
she, only one week less perfect.

Chocolate Box

Late neglected November, Leporello,
and more back-garden rosy-red apples
decorated the tree than countable leaves
when she, through the window,
saw a blue-tit on a bough.

Sighed: 'What an unbelievable pretty picture,
an old-fashioned chocolate box.'

Later, surprised, thinking of unpicked apples,
of course I tasted her red pretty mouth.

Later still, at twilight, the unwrapping.
Her falling black dress rustling
like chocolate-paper;

and the whole delicious
old-fashioned, Rubens-beautiful
box open. Offered and taken: truffle,
cherry liqueur, marzipan, Turkish Delight.

Legacy

Savages adore personal ornament
so take my rose-cut diamond made of glass,
    my brass diadem, my false pearls.

Take my brooch that tries to look like amber,
the earrings you covet, my brummagems.
    Alas, few loaves, fewer fish.

Darling, for you my only brilliants.
For you, my best, my sapphire-like marbles
    plundered from a child's tin box.

My fake gold bangle you may also keep,
that which I won with a wooden ball
    at an Easter fair in Ponty.

I bequeath too my paste-jewel husband.
Bed that bad trickster as you've longed to do —
    my woolworth man, my worthless drag.

Lastly, darling, wear my slave's iron ring.
You'll find beneath its secret bezel
    poison for emergency.

Evergreens

1

'Death? That's for other people,'
Billy Lucas used to say,
sad, sunny-side up, verbal Billy Lucas.

It's winter now in his closed shop-doorway.

He used to roll up his trousers,
dart towards an autumn tree
quicker than a dog-hunted cat
and, at the quivering top, shout out
with spotless joy, 'I am immortal!'

Sometimes he seemed to be
the happiest patient
in that hospital of sorrows.

It's winter now in the grounds of St Ebbas.

The tall deciduous trees have staged
their own phoney funerals
(such morbid, such colourful rehearsals)
and pose for black and white photography.

Who'll cry, 'Long live manic denial,'
esteem the cedar and the yew
and all euphoric Evergreens?

2

It's summer now in the Municipal Gardens.
I know a consoling fountain there. Sssh, surprise:
a cherub, copper greenish-blue, juggles
4 open-mouthed, water-spouting fish. Look! one more
peeing trout has landed between his thighs.

I pass a hoarse-voiced, overbearded crazy
on a wooden bench. It seems that he prays
to this small fat idol who juggles behind
sunlit shatterings of water. The cherub, of course,
smiles on — insouciant and ecstatic and blind.

Shmelke

(For A.B.)

Consider the chassidic story of Shmelke
the wise, the celebrated Shmelke of Nikolsburg:
how he, to be honoured among men,
to be word-oiled and garlanded
at the ceremony of ten
dozen uplifted beards,
demanded, first, a room with a mirror.

Before it he stood, head to toe,
solemnly cooing, 'Lo, you are wonderful, Shmelke,
you are generous and compassionate;
you are an eagle above the stars;
you take root downward, bear fruit upward;
you have the energy of broad rivers;
you leap like a hart over the green herb,
over the grass in the field. You are deft,
seemly, and beautiful of countenance.
Shmelke, you are a paragon of virtue;
you are peerless, flawless, humorous,
spiritual like the orange blossom.
You are a saint, Shmelke, holy, holy, holy,
the earth a mere syllable of your glory.'

Those near the portals observing Shmelke,
overhearing Shmelke, were puzzled, disturbed.

'But I was merely preparing myself
by uttering absurdities to the mirror,'
said Shmelke. 'Now I'm ready for your compliments.
Lead me to the platform, let us proceed.'

Cricket Ball

1935, I watched Glamorgan play
especially Slogger Smart, free
from the disgrace of fame, unrenowned,
but the biggest hit with me.

A three-spring flash of willow
and suddenly, the sound of summer
as the thumped ball, alive, would leave
the applauding ground.

Once, hell for leather, it curled
over the workman's crane
in Westgate Street
to crash, they said, through a discreet
Angel Hotel windowpane.

But I, a pre-war boy,
(or someone with my name)
wanted it, that Eden day,
to scoot around the turning world,
to mock physics and gravity,
to rainbow-arch the posh hotel
higher, deranged, on and on, allegro,
(the Taff a gleam of mercury below)
going, going, gone
towards the Caerphilly mountain range.

Vanishings! The years, too, gone like change.
But the traveling Taff seems the same.
It's late. I peer at the failing sky
over Westgate Street
and wait. I smell cut grass.
I shine an apple on my thigh.

Two Photographs

Here's a photograph of grandmother, Annabella.
How slim she appears, how vulnerable. Pretty.
And here's a photograph of grandmother, Doris.
How portly she looks, formidable. Handsome.
Annabella wears a demure black frock with an amber brooch.
Doris, a lacy black gown with a string of pearls.
One photo's marked *Ystalyfera* 1880,
the other *Bridgend* 1890.
Both were told to say, 'Cheese'; one, defiant, said 'Chalk!'

Annabella spoke Welsh with a Patagonian accent.
Doris spoke English with a Welsh Valleys' lilt.
Annabella fasted — pious, passive, enjoyed small-talk.
Doris feasted — pacy, pushy, would never pray. Ate pork!
When Annabella told Doris she was damned
indecorous Doris devilishly laughed.
I liked Doris, I liked Annabella,
though Doris was bossy and Annabella daft.
I do not think they liked each other.

Last night I dreamed they stood back to back,
not for the commencement of a duel
but to see who was taller! Now, in these revived
waking hours, my Eau de Cologne grandmothers
with buns of gray hair, of withered rose,
seem illusory, fugitive, like my dream —
or like the dust that secretively flows
in a sudden sunbeam (sieved through leaky curtains)
and disappears when and where that sunbeam goes.

Of two old ladies once uxoriously loved,
what's survived? An amber brooch, a string of pearls,
two photographs. Happening on them, my children's

grandchildren will ask 'Who?' — hardly aware
that if this be not true, I never lived.

In the National Gallery

Each single angel is terrible
        R.M. Rilke

Not these, hardly these, not even Piero's
smoothy-faced St Michael, despite big sword
in one hand, nasty snake's head in other;
certainly not the angel Gabriel, mild,
bored with his pose of kneeling and caught again
in the flashlight eyes of wild Fra Lippi:

all said and done, a mere silly, pre-pubertal boy
with a simpering look of 'Gee, you're pregnant!',
overdressed in Sunday-best, peacock's wings
that would not lift him higher than a tree.
And those other angels (God permitting)
who granted impure painters with pure ability

a sitting — how unhappy they appear,
androgynous, holy ones with male names
(designated legends ago, of course, by men)
so tame, surely, that if you cried hosannas,
clapped hands loudly, they'd disappear slowly
back to vast Invisibility.

But that stranger there, so corporeal,
who scowls now at the sweet Virgin of the Rocks,
is he, perhaps, in disguise even to himself,
a descendant of Azazel or Shemhazai?
And others who come in from Trafalgar Square
to be fazed by the fangless spell of moral Art

are they secretly terrible — offspring
of fallen angels and daughters of men:

hair-raising Emim whose glance can stop the heart;
Zamzummim, masters and monsters in war;
Nephilim, called such, since they brought this world
to its still falling fall when they themselves fell?

In the Villa Borghese

The chase. Through the wood, the terror of it.
The choice. Violent love or vegetable asylum.
Still true, sometimes, for uncertain men.
Still true, sometimes, for certain women.
She, with the soul of a nun, chose.

In the Villa Borghese they have become marble.
Millions of days, millions of nights
they pose. He, too, ironically petrified.

With a stethoscope I want to hear
their two hearts beat within the marble.
I want to put a mirror to their mouths.

According to Ovid, she chose. Who cried?
She left him priapic and aching.
Did it rain then? Did he lift his god's leg?

Now I hear, outside, the seminal patter of it
on wide laurel leaves. No matter,
a tree might welcome such fresh drenching.

A feminist victory? Hardly.
True, one more heavy breather denied —
unless, of course, Ovid, pleasing some prim,
some god-loving, soma-loathing priest,
sweetened an older, raunchier story. Lied.

Destinies

(*To Francis Celoria*)

Sometimes the gods appear to be insane.
So addicted to metamorphosis!
Pity the unloved vulture flying above a roof,
pity the lone eagle settling on a mountain.

Long ago, 'Hail Periphas!' cried the populace
and built a great temple in his honour;
began to call him, 'Overlooker of All'
and at the agora, 'Your Imperial Grace',

offending big-jawed Zeus. His boss-face gorged
with anger — he, flash lord of the thunderbolts,
scandalous incinerator of men —
bridled his ten white horses and charged

over boiling plains toward the Aegean shore
where that afternoon, in sand-dune amour,
Periphas, anastomosing with Phene, sighed,
'Dear one,' while she replied, 'Love evermore!'

Four times unignorable Zeus tapped
the busy bare back of rapt Periphas.
Alas, when Periphas turned he was turned
into a bird, into an eagle that flapped

its wings till Phene, flushed, opened her eyes.
First, surprise. Then appalling cries were heard;
but still she, faithful wife, begged to become
bird also. 'Please Judicious One, All-wise.'

Praised, the god, red-toothed, smiled. Would he concur?
Her nakedness fled and she was covered
with feathers till, heart and head, Phene was
all bird, all sorry-looking vulture.

The sweetness of feminine self-denial!
Are male saints, unmasked, deceiving women?
Other men become wolves to savage other men
so who'd arraign Zeus? Put the gods on trial?

They pester with vipers the sleep of mankind
and, like men, won't forgive those they've injured.
What horrors have they in mind, what transformations
in the zoo of Time to come? To prove unkind?

Sometimes the gods cannot remain aloof
when the populace love a man too much.
Pity the lone eagle flying about a mountain.
Pity the unloved vulture settling on a roof.

Just One of Those Days, William

Back from your id-holiday in Greece,
closing the front door behind you,
oh unlikely omen, your left foot stepped
on the silence of an ant. Deleted!
Just one of those days, William.

Soon after, you passed the Reservoir,
saw a crow flying with seagulls,
taking off when they did, trying
to alight when they did, desperate
to float on water — defeated.

Then, at the office, the Three appeared.
You were bugged. They knew your liaison
with Lais. Demanded drachmas,
and clicked their castrating scissors.
Just one of those days, William,

like that when naughty Icarus,
ignoring his father's advice
(the old taboo), dared illicit elevation —
wild on a high, happy as vice,
till he felt both wings shift, unglue;

like that when cissy Narcissus
espied a pretty boy in the pool
(the insolence of imitation!).
The fool drowned trying to embrace him.
Just one of those days, William.

Lunchtime, unmerry in 'The Bear',
you waited hours for the waiters,
Agrius and Orius. Each weighed a ton.

They sat in the cockroached kitchen,
big teeth chewing more than a bun.

Back at the office, you found faeces on
the Turkish carpet, drawers flung open,
phone wires cut, oak desk smashed,
and, uninsured, the Golden Fleece gone.
Just one of those days, William,

like that when Zeus descended — uncouth,
hauled Periphas off nude Phene,
then turned those lovers into birds:
he, an eagle to the mountain,
she, a vulture to the roof;

like that when bare-chested Hylas
while rowing across the river
was dragged below the water
by nymphomaniacal nymphs.
Just one of those days, William.

And they talk of Sod's malicious law,
the wincing unease of not knowing
what you have long forgotten,
and that as you are to an ant,
someone, Someone, may be to you.

Touch Wood

Come, let us praise wood
no longer agrestial.
Not the trillions of coffins
but wood within a living house,
the quietude of an empty bookcase,
the loneliness of scattered chairs —
the metamorphosis
of trees, shrubs, bushes, twigs.
Doors particularly, upstairs, downstairs,
whatever their disposition,
welcoming, half open,
or secretively shut.

It does not matter.
Delightful the craftsmanship
of their lintels,
so comely, so pleasant,
like the repeated oblongs
of windowframes, upstairs, downstairs,
like the serenity of windowsills
that carry vases, flower-pots.
And who could not respond
to the utilitarian elegance
of a wide staircase
rising from a parquet floor?

What a history wood has,
what old echoing stories
in the random museum of the mind:
the gopher ark of Noah
floating high above the mountains;
the huge, staring Trojan horse;
Diogenes's fat barrel;

Horatius's one-way bridge
that fell into the Tiber;
King Arthur's Round Table —
all these relics lost forever
like Jesus's insensate Cross.

Sometimes I think we should construct
in the garden of a living house
an idol of various woods:
head of Lombardy Poplar,
trunk of reliable Oak,
arms of Elm and Pine,
hands of Lime and Plane,
legs of Birch and Beech,
feet of grainy Sycamore
and genitals (of course, discreet)
of musty Fig tree, untidy Fir
and the droopy Weeping Willow.

November nights when we're asleep,
when unbuttoned winds shake the house,
what the spirit of the house
if not the spirit of the forest?
What replies if not primal wood,
dryad-ghost and Daphne-creak,
wild cries of wood awakening?
We, stern-faced as mourners, slumber on,
carry in dream the golden bough
from some black forgotten tree
of the windless underworld
back to the leaf-strewn morning.

Blessings and Curses

1 *Sunflowers*

I

Near the back-garden's West wall,
near a synagogue shemozzle of wasps
about michaelmas daisies,
a watchful congregation
of sunflowers in their Sunday best.

Guests of autumn, they too
are enslaved by religion.
Not Jewish or Moslem flowers these:
they pray to the sun,
turn to the South. Obsessed.

II

They do not hear her footsteps.
Choosing, she cuts twelve tall stems.
Held close, the green leaves curl
to the curve of her breast.

Chosen, no apostles these.
Stripped of their leaves, half undressed,
stiff with hubris, their anther-buttons
seem more blatantly manifest.
Twelve glorious atheists
free of the sun's power,
the tyranny of the sun.

The full vase an inflorescence of yellow,
an unashamed zest of yellow,

a musical purity of yellow,
and merely by admiring we are blessed.

2 *November Bonfire*

After the sunset ignited windows
then faded, the sky-dangle of fireworks.
Rockets whoosh towards haughty stars
from our acrid back-garden.
Each year the funeral pomp of autumn,
and soon we blaze up a log-fire
to incinerate a scarecrow.
Welcome, you pilgrims of light.
Sing, everybody, sing. Sing louder.
Why follow the arrow
of the huge blind archer?
Sing dirges for mortuary golden rods,
orisons for cadavers of sunflowers,
and higher and higher the log-fire.
Where else did the sunset go?

Now the children dance around it,
small corybants around it,
the singing and singing louder,
prancing dwarf shadows around it
to ward off inquisitive demons.
Light of the unlocked flames,
crack of the sparks flying,
heat of the timbers' alkalines.
Look! Listen! Feel! Sing! Dance!
The scarecrow's burning alive,
opening its mouth but once;
then, into ash, it collapses.

Hallelujah! Hallelujah! —
till all smell of wood-smoke,
till all, touch wood, be blessed.

3 *Solace*

On her deathbed my spunky mother
wishing to be left alone, not helped,
cursed me. My hand, mid-air, still as stone.
Her sudden gritty voice jarring and unjust,
a snarling stranger's voice, sister of one
who knew the 32 curses of Leviticus.
The Dukes of Edom would have been amazed,
the Mighty of Moab would have been undone.

That night each man cursed became my brother.

Today I read how Rabbi Simeon's son
had been vilely cursed: *May your permanent*
home be ruined, may your temporary
abodes be built up. 'These are blessings not
curses,' Simeon interpreted, cocksure.
'You are wished Long Life so that your own plot
in the family cemetery be ruined,
and the houses wherein you live endure.'

Sunday Night, Monday Morning

Not like the vandal wind outside
upturning trees, wooden park-seats.
Call me subtle, a click half-heard
opening or closing interior doors.

Upstairs, you open both your eyes,
sit up in bed, listening. Only a show
of moon-shadows, vague. Your head sinks
on a sinking pillow. Goodbye clock.

Your sleeping mind has timeless caves
where extinct creatures snore and stir.
I'm home there, like a troglodyte.
I'll find a Cuvier bone for you.

I'll paint dawn murals, you shall dream them.
(Asleep, how much does your breathing weigh?
The air above the clouds is heavier.)
Erotic one, throw high your silver stick.

Ho! A procession: unicorns (how chic),
tall soothsayers, red-gowned Chaldeans
with golden chains about their necks.
They follow you to morning's abattoir.

You draw the curtains back, I'm still here,
your aide-mémoire, your compass-needle,
your master that some call revenant
(quiet as the spider in the bath).

By what I am, know what you do.
You turn tap steam on, exit spider,
(some apocalypse, some aubade)
you wipe the mirror clear of dream.

Thankyou Note

for the unbidden swish of morning curtains
you opened wide — letting sleep-baiting shafts
of sunlight enter to lie down by my side;
for adagio afternoons when you did the punting
(my toiling eyes researched the shifting miles of sky);
for back-garden evenings when you chopped the wood
and I, incomparably, did the grunting;
(a man too good for this world of snarling
is no good for his wife — truth's the safest lie);

for applauding my poetry, O most perceptive spouse;
for the improbable and lunatic, my darling;
for amorous amnesties after rancorous rows
like the sweet-nothing whisperings of a leafy park
after the blatant noise of a city street
(exit booming cannons, enter peaceful ploughs);
for kindnesses the blind side of my night-moods;
for lamps you brought in to devour the dark.

On the Evening Road

A disgrace a man of my age
to have come this far and not to know;
the fields inert with ignorant mist,
the road between, lost, unsignposted.

I may as well sing a little
since no-one's around to hear me,
'The Song of Omega' my father sang
though the words I've mostly forgotten.

I may as well dance a bit, too,
since no-one's around to scold me:
'Disgrace, a man of his age singing
drunkenly — not knowing where he is.'

Now the Caladrius bird lands
as it must, on the road ahead of me
and drops its dung. Turn towards me, bird,
O turn, turn, with your yellow beak.

Arcadia, One Mile

O Taste and See

Because of a kiss on the forehead
in the long Night's infirmary,
through the red wine let light shine deep.

Because of the thirtysix just men
that so stealthily roam this earth
raise high the glass and do not weep.

Who says the world is not a wedding?
Couples, in their oases, lullabye.
Let glass be full before they sleep.

Toast all that which seems to vanish
like a rainbow stared at, those bright
truant things that will not keep;

and ignorance of the last night
of our lives, its famished breathing.
Then, in the red wine, taste the light.

The Maestro

'I'll portray you with flutes, oboes and harp.'
So Schumann to Clara. As I would you.

Now, in this front room of a tree-repeated street,
I practise mere stumbling tunes. But the maestro
behind me, in the mirror, my discreet double,
plays your music's parables flawlessly,
Schumann-like, strange and tragical and sweet.

At the Albert Hall

Anarchic dissonances first, so that
somewhere else a lonely scarecrow shivers
in a winter field. A mortician's crow
perches on its head. It begins to snow.
They bring the scarecrow indoors. They feed it
with phosphorus so it should glow at night.
A great orchestra's tuning-up is ghost talk.

The wand! Then the sudden tamed silence of
a cemetery. Who dares to blackly cough?
Threatened, the conductor raises both arms,
an invisible gun pressed to his back.
Listen. And they speak of the sweet psalmist
of Israel, of 200 loaves of bread
and of 100 bundles of raisins.

The Musical Express

A boy like you, he had said (1946)
will end up on the Musical Express.

What did that Swiss Cottage refugee,
that graphologist from Vienna
who had escaped the sealed wagons
mean?

I looked at my own handwriting
as if it were a mirror,
saw only a frosted window.

Did he refer merely to symphonic music's
totalitarian finale,
how loudly it accelerates towards silence?

My allegro days are here now:
one morning vast cloudless heaven
unautographed
full of someone else's Forever;
the next, when I blink,
another day, another season,
the stern modesties of a Welsh sky.

You'll end up, son, on the Musical Express.

Rain or shine, days track by so fast now
I can't read the stations' names
that I'm passing through.

One long slanting afternoon,
travelling in the U.S.A. when I was young,
first I saw a road sign:

ARCADIA, ONE MILE,
then a line of automobiles
all with headlights on,
coming towards me at mourning pace.

Et in Arcadia ego.

Consider the eyes of baby Hitler
new born, a colourless blue,
that graphologist had said.
Like yours were. Like mine.

Why should I tell you more?
Some touch wood and some stone touches
and a fool is his own informer,
autobiography a form of suicide.

He spoke adagio, that survivor,
— adagio molto espressivo —
and I, so lucky, knew how
the half-sleeping mind has many caves
and a man's country, too, is his fate.

Photograph and White Tulips

A little nearer please. And a little nearer
we move to the window, to the polished table.
Objects become professional: mannequins
preening themselves before an audience. Only
the tulips, self-absorbed, ignore the camera.

All photographs flatter us if we wait
long enough. So we awkwardly Smile please
while long-necked tulips, sinuous out of the vase,
droop over the polished table. They're entranced
by their own puffed and smudgy reflections.

Hold it! Click. Once more! And we smile again
at one who'll be irrevocably absent.
Quick. Be quick! the tulips, like swans, will dip
their heads deep into the polished table
frightening us. Thank you. And we turn thinking,

What a fuss! Yet decades later, dice thrown,
we'll hold it, thank you, this fable of gone
youth (was that us?) and we shall smile please
and come a little nearer to the impetuous
once-upon-a-time that can never be twice.

(Never never be twice!) Yet we'll always recall
how white tulips, quick quick, changed into swans
enthralled, drinking from a polished table.
As for those white petals, they'll never fall
in that little black coffin now carrying us.

The Boasts of
Hywel ab Owain Gwynedd

(12th century)

Sunday, skilled in zealous verse I praise the Lord.
Monday, I sing in bed to my busty Nest,
'Such whiteness you are, pear blossom must be jealous.'
Tuesday, scholar Gwladus. Not to love her is a sin.
My couplets she pigeon-coos when I thrust to woo her
till her pale cheeks flush like rosy apple skin.
Wednesday, Generys. Dry old hymns I steal to please her.
Then with passion fruit in season I kneel to ease her.
Thursday, Hunydd, no hesitating lady, she.
One small cherry-englyn and she's my devotee.
Friday, worried Hawis, my epic regular.
She wants no baby, she's gooseberry vehement
till sugared by my poetry of endearment.
Saturday, I score and score. One tidy eulogy
and I'm away — I can't brake — through an orchard
I adore. O sweet riot of efflorescence,
let her name be secret for her husband's sake,
my peach of a woman, my vegetarian diet.

O tongue, lick up juices of the fruit. O teeth
— I've all of mine — be sure my busy tongue keeps quiet.

Lament of Heledd

(based on a fragment of a 9th century Welsh saga poem)

I

I had four brothers. A pike upholds the head
of noble Cynddylan. The corn is red.

I had four brothers. Cynon and Gwiawn
butchered in the straw, their swords not drawn.

Four brothers I had. Vague, hesitant Gwyn
last to fall. Through his neck a javelin.

When will this brute night end? Where shall I go?
Morning's mortuary will be kitchen for the crow.

II

Cynddylan's Hall is dark tonight.
The stone stairs lead nowhere. No candle glows
behind the lower then the higher windows.

Cynddylan's Hall is dark tonight
and dark the smoke rising from its ruin.
Slain, slain, are Cynddylan and all our kin.

Cynddylan's Hall is dark tonight,
its great roof burnt down, I can see the stars.
Curse those Englishmen, their bloody wars.

Cynddylan's Hall is dark tonight.
No orison is wailed to harp or lute.
O ghost brothers, your sister's destitute.

Cynddylan's Hall is dark tonight,
its silence outrageous. I shall go mad.
I smell skeletons. O blood of my blood.

Cynddylan's Hall is dark tonight.
Should I live on? I am no heroine.
O Cynddylan, Cynon, Gwiawn, and Gwyn.

Welsh Valley Cinema, 1930s

In The Palace of the slums,
from the Saturday night pit,
from an unseen shaft of darkness
I remember it: how, first, a sound
took wing grandly; then the thrill
of a fairground sight — it rose,
lordly stout thing, boasting
a carnival of gaudy-bright,
changing colours while wheezing out
swelling rhonchi of musical asthma.

I hear it still, played with panache
by renowned gent, Cathedral Jones,
'When the Broadway Baby Says Goodnight
it's Early in the Morning' — then he and it
sank to disappear, a dream underground.

Later, those, downstairs, gobbing silicosis
(shoeless feet on the mecca carpet),
observed a miracle — the girl next door,
a poor ragged Goldilocks,
dab away her glycerine tears
to kiss cuff-linked Cary Grant
under an elegance of chandeliers.
(No files on Cary. No holes in *his* socks.)

And still the Woodbine smoke swirled on
in the opium beam of the operator's box
till THE END — of course, upbeat.
Then from The Palace, the damned Fall,
the glum, too silent trooping out
into the trauma of paradox:
the familiar malice of the dreary,

unemployed, gas-lamped street
and the striking of the small Town's clocks.

Sixth-Form Poet

When my acne almost cleared
I fell in love with humankind.
I wanted to requisition Poetry,
a revolution in my mind.

To the barricades not the court,
my gorgeous rage would console.
Though love be blind it sees
with the optic nerve of the soul.

Poetry is written in the brain
but the brain is bathed in blood.
I sang no praises for the King,
I, laureate to Robin Hood.

A Political Prisoner

'Franco could have freed Miguel Hernandez from prison.
How could a shepherd boy used to living in the open air
live seven years in prison. He got T.B. His execution was
carried out by Tuberculosis.' Neruda

1

The noise of many knuckles on metal,
we do not hear it.
There is lightning when we are asleep
and thunder that does not speak;
there are guitars without strings
and nightingales with tongues of glass.

Yet even if we imagine it,
the metal sound of bolts shut to,
then feet stamping down echoing corridors,
what can we do who stroll on easy grass,
who smile back at the gracious and the
goodlooking?

Righteous the rhetoric of indignation,
but protesting poems, like the plaster angels,
are impotent. They commit no crimes,
they pass no laws; they grant amnesty
only to those who, in safety, write them.

2

Shepherd from the village, Orihuela,
who, whistling, could mimic different birds,
who, by day, would count the cabra,

by night, from the hills, the straying stars,
you opened your eyelids noiselessly,
found you were sitting, hunched in a cell.
You howled, hurled a bucket at the bars.

Far from the villanelle of nightingales
or the sexual moan in the throat of doves,
they handed you a bible, remarked slyly,
'Poet, feel at home.' Then Hell's Time
seemed to strike its palindrome note
and you knew you would perish in that cell.
'Flesh falls off gradually,
bones collapse suddenly,' you wrote.

3

Within the towering walls of every gray jail,
especially at night, the desire to escape
from the clock's small thefts. Maybe for you, too,
once, after lights out, it was carnival time:
drums beating, somersaulting clowns, men on stilts,
each wearing a bull's mask meant to chill,
and lewd codpieces of unnatural size.
Then the coloured carts and their pretty lanterns,
marching girls in skimpy skirts, bare lifting thighs,
fire-swallowers and those with a juggling skill.

Surely they came, moving pictures, floating
like pointillist dust in substantial moonbeams,
through your cramped cell — though vanishing at dawn
when all the birds that ever were, near and remote,
did not sweetly sing or corvine croak; but coughed,
as you did, spills of bacilli and blood.

The stinking vultures! The pterodactyls!

'You threw me a lemon, it was sour,' you wrote.

C'est La Vie Politique

When promised
a subtle perfume,
tactful dilutions
of musk, civet, ambergris,

expect 'a human error',
a veritable gasworks.
Dry in the polluted air
plain H_2S.

When promised
a hundred-piece orchestra —
Berlioz, Mahler —
a tune on a comb.

When a Queen's diamond,
a snail's shell;
when a King's golden crown,
a funny paper hat.

Consider Mr Maltby,
fancy tailor, who agreed
a suicide pact
with his wife.

She did not falter;
he was unable.
He propped her up
naked in the bath.

Night after night
brought lit candles
into that bathroom
where he quietly dined,

faithfully choosing
her favourite dishes,
fish mainly — turbot, trout —
gently removing the bones.

Refugee

What is the name of your country?
    Its frontiers keep changing.
What is the Capital of your country?
    The town where blood issued
    through the cold and hot water taps.
What is your National Anthem?
    The ancient fugue of screams.
Who are your compatriots?
    The crippled, the groping blinded,
    the wan dead not yet in their dungeons.
Who is your leader?
    Death's trumpet-tongued fool.
What is the name of your son?
    Despair.
What is the name of your daughter?
    Derangement.
Why is your husband not with you?
    He raised high the pleading
    white flag of surrender.

A Heritage

A heritage of a sort.
A heritage of comradeship and suffocation.

The bawling pit-hooter and the god's
explosive foray, vengeance, before retreating
to his throne of sulphur.

Now this black-robed god of fossils
and funerals,
petrifier of underground forests
and flowers,
emerges with his grim retinue
past a pony's skeleton, past human skulls,
into his half-propped up, empty, carbon colony.

Above, on the brutalized,
unstitched side of a Welsh mountain,
it has to be someone from somewhere else
who will sing solo

not of the marasmus of the Valleys,
the pit-wheels that do not turn,
the pump-house abandoned;

nor of how, after a half-mile fall
regiments of miners' lamps
no longer, midge-like,
rise and slip and bob.

Only someone uncommitted,
someone from somewhere else,
panorama-high on a coal-tip,
may jubilantly laud

the re-entry of the exiled god
into his shadowless kingdom.

He, drunk with methane,
raising a man's femur like a scepter;
she, his ravished queen,
admiring the blood-stained black roses
that could not thrive on the plains of Enna.

Altercation in Splott

Before the frosted window is shattered
immigrant, touch stone and be lucky.

Widower, Sunil, calls most men, 'Sir.'
Hindu pacifist, chanter of prayers.

Cold and cloned, the next door room to his:
bed, chair, threadbare carpet, vertical

fat coffin with a keyhole in it,
damp stain of almost Wales on the wall,

inert with the slow interminable
silence of a broken radio

till volcano-loud, football hooligan,
Darren Jones, big-boots in. Me? Racialist?

Nah. Politics is shit, mun. On the stairs
I smiles back at the Paki, see.

But rust sleeps within the iron.
One night, pub closed, Darren's jugular.

Paki, you wanker, stop chantin', Christ!
Nothin' much, see. Bust 'is 'ead in a bit

that's all. No shit under the door like.
Righteous as a Town Hall, Darren Jones.

One winter week's notice for bleak Sunil.
Never complain to a blue-eyed landlord.

Ice is on the pond. Swan is on the snow.
But far from the neighbourhood of parks,

Sunil, long-armed, suitcase in each hand,
treads past the depot on pavements' linen,

seems, in sleet-mist, more a conjuration
than a man. Indian out of season.

Sir, stone falls on jug: woe.
Sir, jug falls on stone: woe.

Assimilation

Even the Sodomites, I said, would allow
distraught refugees into their desert city,
provide them with a Sodom-made bed.

But strangers too tall, it must be admitted,
had their legs chopped off; and nationalistic Sods
heaved at heads and feet of those too small
till beds and bodies beautifully fitted.

Souls

'After the last breath, eyelids must be closed
quickly. For eyes are windows of the soul
— that shy thing which is immortal. And none
should see its exit vulnerably exposed,'

proclaimed the bearded man on Yom Kippur.
Grown-ups believed in the soul. Otherwise
why did grandfather murmur the morning prayer,
'Lord, the soul Thou hast given me is pure'?

Near the kitchen door where they notched my height
a mirror hung. There I saw the big eyes
of a boy. I could not picture the soul
immaterial and immortal. A cone of light?

Those two black zeros the soul's windows? Daft!
Later, at medical school, I learnt of
the pineal gland, its size a cherry-stone,
vestige of the third eye, and laughed.

But seven colours hide in light's disguise
and the blue sky's black. No wonder Egyptians
once believed, in their metamorphosis,
souls soared, became visible: butterflies.

Now old, I'm credulous. Superstition clings.
After the melting eyes and devastation
of Hiroshima, they say butterflies, crazed,
flew about, fluttering soundless things.

My Neighbour, Itzig

My neighbour, Itzig,
has gone queer with religion.
Yesterday he asked me
who named the angels!

Today his dog is barking and barking.

But like music that's ceased
in an adjoining room
Itzig is not here.
He is nowhere else, either.

Itzig, listen, your dog needs a walk.

But Itzig is droning on and on
— open the window, someone —
a prayer archaic and musty
and full of O.

His sad feet are on this earth,
his happy head is elsewhere
among the configuration
of the 7 palaces of light.

Come back, Itzig, your dog needs feeding.

But Itzig quests for the 8th colour.
His soul is cartwheeling, he's far
from the barely manageable
drama of the Present Tense.

Come back, Itzig, your dog needs water.

But Itzig follows, with eyes closed,
the footsteps of the sages
Amora and Rehumai
who never existed.

A Letter from Ogmore-by-Sea

Goodbye, 20th Century.
What should I mourn?
Hiroshima? Auschwitz?
Our friend, Carmi, said,
'Thank forgetfulness
else we could not live;
thank memory
else we'd have no life.'

Goodbye, 20th Century.
What shall I celebrate?
Darling, I'm out of date:
even my nostalgia
is becoming history.
Those garish, come-on posters
outside a cinema,
announce the Famous
I've never heard of.
So many other friends, too,
now like Carmi, have joined
a genealogy of ghosts.

But here, this mellow evening,
on these high cliffs I look down
to read the unrolling
holy scrolls of the sea. They are
blank. The enigma is alive
and, for the Present, I boast,
thumbs in lapels, I survive.

Delightful Eros
still hauls Reason along
zig-zag on a taut leash.

I'm still unsettled by
the silence in framed pictures,
foreground and background;
or the mastery of music
over mind. And I hail
the world within a word.
I do not need to be
a fabulist like Iolo
who, from this same coast,
would see seven sails
where there was but one.

Goodbye, 20th Century,
your trumpets and your drums,
your war-wounds still unhealed.
Goodbye, I-must-leave-you-Dolly,
goodbye Lily Marlene.
Has the Past always a future?
Will there always be
a jackboot on the stair,
a refugee to roam?
A man with no roots is lost
like the darkness in the forest
and it costs 100 years
for a hiding place
to become a home.

Now secular strangers come
sealed in Fords and Nissans,
a congregation of cars,
to this opening estuary
so various, so beautiful, so old.
The tide is out.
And from the reeled-
in sea — not from
the human mind's vexed fathoms —

the eternal, murderous,
fanged Tusker Rock is revealed.

An Interrupted Letter

In this room's winterlight the travail of
a letter to a new widow. Solemn,
the increasing enterprise of age.
I stutter. Consoling words come slow,
seem false, as if spoken on a stage.
It would be easier to send flowers.

I think of her closing her husband's eyelids
and I look up. Siberian snow hesitated,
then parachuted into our garden
for hours, confiscating yesterday's
footprints. Shall I send flowers?

But now my wife, unaware in the far kitchen,
suddenly sings, captivating me,
my pen mid-air above a muffled page.

When we were young, tremulant with Spring,
often off-key she'd sing her repertoire —
dateless folk songs, dance tunes dated.
In her Pears-suds bath I'd hear her,
in the Morris Minor with our kids.

I must return to my hiemal letter.
Sing on love, as once you did, sing and sing
for past youth, for hungers unabated.

Useful Knowledge

Shy Colin, the most silent of men
despite his ammunition of facts.
He'd bomb them out at dinner parties
before signing off from conversation.

'The mastrich tree, as you probably know,
is brown, resinous, and most fragrant.'
'Volapuk? Nobody speaks it now.
Lost its one thousand, five hundred words.'

At Anne's, he said, 'Tortoises often die
from diphtheria.' At our place, he told us
'Lake Titicaca's half the size of Wales —
half's in Bolivia, half in Peru.'

Last April, when his two year old son
lay big-eyed in The Royal Infirmary,
Colin heard the consultant whisper
to his Registrar, 'Nieman-Pick Disease.'

Colin closed his eyes, cried out shrilly,
'A genetically determined disorder
where splenectomy is palliative.
Death occurs quite early during childhood.'

Alzheimer's

Absolutely nothing
8 jars of nothing
And 1 jar of barley sugar
    2 jars of acid drops
    3 jars of chocolate drops
    4 jars of liquorice allsorts
    5 jars of mintoes
    6 jars of humbugs
    7 jars of bulls' eyes.

An old-age adagio, cello-sad.
Suspicions, accusations,
whisperings of the profane,
the enthronement of doubt.
Then a turning back,
light blue, dark blue, purple,
to the bleak mechanism.
Aphasia, agnosia,
a blank 75" record, black
like the far farmhouse
that merges with
night-surrounding fields
when the electric
in the high bedroom
at last goes out.

And 7 jars of bulls' eyes
    6 jars of humbugs
    5 jars of mintoes
    4 jars of liquorice allsorts
    3 jars of chocolate drops
    2 jars of acid drops
    1 jar of barley sugar

8 jars of nothing
absolutely nothing

Child Drawing in a Hospital Bed

Any child can open wide
the occult doors of a colour
naively to call, 'Who's there?'
For this sick girl drawing
outstep invisible ones
imprisoned everywhere.
Wasp on a windowpane.

Darkest tulip her head bends,
face white as leukaemia,
till the prince in his tower,
on parole from a story,
descends by royal crayon
and, thrilled, stays half an hour.
Wasp on a windowpane.

Birds of Rhiannon, pencilled,
alight to wake the dead —
they do not sing, she rubs them out,
they smudge into vanishings,
they swoop to Nowhere
as if disturbed by a shout.
Wasp on a windowpane.

Omens. Wild astrologies whirl:
sun and moon begin to soar.
Unlikely that maroon sky
green Christmas trees fly through
— doctors know what logic's for.
Tell me, what is magic for?
Wasp on a windowpane.

Now penal-black she profiles

four eerie malformed horses,
nostrils tethered to the ground.
Unperturbed, the child attends
for one to uplift its neck
and turn its death's head round.
Wasp on a windowpane.

Thomas Girtin's 'The White House'

Something odd about the house — so luminous
as if a truant god were resting there.

And those daffodil-bordered clouds seem intent
to spill but will, of course, never. Their oblique
presentiments of rain, their pollutions of smoke
behind, above, a huge icon of a windmill.

Though such painted scenes reject the future,
and quarrel with the ghost of Heraclitus,
now, sleep-walking into Girtin's numinous
mastery of a moment, I want narrative.

I want to forecast what the weather will bring
but all the clocks within that spotlit house,
the effulgent white house on the promontory,
have stopped at the mood of eternal evening.

The contrary sky cannot play its mobiles;
no chill wind can turn around the cross
of this indisposed windmill or stir the still
waters, the fishing boats, their capsized doubles.

I want to smell something more than paint. Loud Life!
its shyest flowers that must be held so close
before their scent is known. Life's armpits, too!
I'm troubled by the silence of this river view.

I want to trick the picture fast-forward,
shake it like a watch to make Time's nothings tick;
let the yawning god quit the house perplexed;
the complacent winds to be vexed again;

anaesthetised fishermen to go home unsurprised
to empty firegrates or expectant wives.

The Stonebreaker

Dear Inchbold,
                    I want you to know about this.

23 miles from London I was walking
with Black Spot when I lingered to gaze at
a steep scarp of the chalky Downs.
I gazed and gazed until I seemed to stand
                    just outside Eden.

Faraway, the beech trees in their summer
magnificence while, nearby, there happened to be
a pile of stones and a barely living tree.
It sprang out of a dead one.

                    Oh Inchbold,
do you believe in the Resurrection?

Remember mild Tom, the model who died,
the one who resembled my young brother?
Suddenly, from nowhere, he appeared
and, with a noiseless hammer, struck the stones.
He did not look pathetic like the Stonebreaker
portrayed by Henry Wallis but wore fake,
unsoiled, peasant's clothes.

                    Before I could speak
a bullfinch alighted on a high branch
of the strange, frail tree and Tom vanished.

You doubt what I saw? I doubt what I saw.
So much is mirage and shadow. The law
of gravity asserts itself in my mind.
I know the far hills are not really blue,

that sunlight does not truly paint the grass
an indistinct yellow. Love, itself, errs.
A child's swift daubs on paper are not Art
though the mother may think so.

Oh Inchbold,
did I see what I saw? Tom breaking stones?

I beg you, tell no-one of this. You know
how some believe we artists are crazy!
Besides, I may paint this experience though
Ruskin says mine is mirror's work not man's.
Write me soon. Your loving friend,

John Brett.

In the Welsh National Museum

(*To Josef Herman*)

Josef, in your thaumaturgic studio,
long live cobalt blue and brown!
Autumn is your season,
twilight is your hour.

Now, in my hometown, you, spooky,
conjure up, abracadabra,
this melancholy impostor
who steals my name.

Is he listening to someone
beyond the picture's frame,
playing a Chopin piano
of autumnal unhappiness?

Josef, this other is not me.
This golem hardly looks like me.
Is this your unbegotten brother
lost in menstrual blood?

If so, his passport (forged)
would have been Polish,
his exile inevitable,
his wound undescribable.

Look! My best brown coat
not yet patched at the elbow,
my cobalt blue shirt
not yet frayed at the collar.

As if challenged he, dire,
(Passport? Colour of wound?)
stares back — that look of loss —
at whomsoever stares at him.

Or across at Augustus John's
too respectable W.H. Davies,
at prettified Dylan Thomas
whose lips pout for a kiss.

Infelicitous! Wrong! Impostors
spellbound, enslaved in their world,
with no *emeth* on their foreheads,
without speech, without pneuma.

But the Welsh say, 'Whoever stares long
at his portrait will, with dismay, see
the devil.' So who's wearing my clothes?
Josef, I know your magic. I'll not stay.

Deaf Men Singing

(To Gillian)

Most poems, like golems, turn to dust at dawn
but you hallow the coarse endeavor, attend
the awkward, the not winging, the also-rans;
cheer Z because it's last; salute deaf men singing
who feel a piano's wood to hear its song,
myopic painters, their details clearly wrong,
their vast perspectives to a No-Man's Past.

Inhuman angels may command perfection
but the hollow circle drawn by Giotto
would have been more genial if hand had wavered.
So you commend sweet error, would not mend
the nervous junction, convert the letter O
to Death's infrangible and favoured number,
with its unseen beginning, no evident end.

Domestic

You need not be cross, why are you
cross-examining me?

By Ishara, queen of the oaths,
hear me out
— let's contend no more, love —

by Ishtar of Nineveh,
by Ishtar of Hattarina,

— do not shout,
what so wild as words are? —

by the hypertensive lord of Wars,
by St Elmo and by Santa Claus,

after the doors of dawn re-opened
— let's cease our battling, love —

I was still bloody-well rattling
bars of a stationary lift
between electrically-lit, empty floors.

To His Friend's Wife

No letters, no photos, no keepsake.

No whistling of a coded tune,
no signals of lover to his lass.

I think you're glad I didn't
when the sea surrendered to the moon.

No scratches, no love-bites, no heartache.

I think I'm glad I didn't
when the church clock tolled the hour.

Your ring shone muffled gold not wanton brass.

Judgement Night we'll not shuffle
to the bench, bent, crass, trembling,
beg pardon, your honour.

We'll stand there upright, alas.

New Granddaughter

You don't know the score, what's you, what's not.
Remote ancestors return you can't disown.
This prelude, this waiting for an encore.

Is that raised hand yours, this wind-pecked morning?
Enigmatic trees, askew, shake above the pram.
All's perplexity, green reverie, shadowland.

But why this grandfatherly spurt of love?
Your skin is silk, your eyes suggest they're blue.
I bend to smell small apricots and milk.

Did I dream that legend of the Angel
who falls to touch each baby's fontanelle
and wipe out racial memory, leaving *déjà vu*?

I'm confessing! Your newness, petite, portends
my mortality — a rattle for you, the bell for me.
Hell, I'm old enough to mutter blessings.

The determinates of the clock increase.
Sometimes you close your eyes noiselessly, turn
your head, listening to music that has ceased.

Presences

I'm halted by the unintentional
honeyed malice of mementos:
this awkward night-school painting
by my genial father-in-law;
this vast desk my mother fussed
to give me. 'Fit for an emperor!'

And here's another hook to chin:
a door opens in the next room
and I hear a snatch of Gershwin —
that tune our car-bound family used
to sing. On music's heartless beat
my keen dead come marching in.

O button-holing familiars,
your blurs I sense, your ashes I taste.
So much I owe, so much forgotten
that I owe. But now dear ghosts go
that I may live. Be brief guests.
Leave with a burglar's haste.

The future's future is another place
where other absences will sting; where
some unfocussed progeny perhaps
will summon me, stumbling on
some inherited thing or, less likely,
reading this poem, maybe!

Last Lunch

In memory of David Wright

That last late lunch we had in Soho
you spoke of friends who had gone before,
edgy prisoners of poetry.

Would readers forget their astute verse-skill,
Jock Graham, Tom Blackburn, Stevie,
who taking the maverick route

from a poisoned tree made a table
and, at that table, ate its fruit?

Then you said, 'My turn, Dannie',
reaching for the bill.

Why Angels Disappeared

When first the celestial orchestra played
decorously the angels began to dance.

This was the time when the moon unmuzzled
glowed twice more luminously than now.

But wanton Azazel, the angel of Vice,
unhooked his nice masterpiece wings, displayed,

enticed daft angels to swig double-strength nectar,
deft angels to juggle the fruits of Paradise.

Hallelujah! Hallelujah! That unquiet night
(such an orgy) half the angels got laid

and their pet unicorns ran riot, began to bite,
called for pale maidens to make life rosier.

Their randy horns grew and grew. Some howled at
the moon, some crapped on the ambrosia.

Soon the Archangel's police arrived, blew
whistles for music to cease, moonlight to fade

and foolishly fed the frenetic unicorns
tinned human flesh, calming pesticides.

Later, the angels ate all the unicorns,
suffered CJD. Not one of them survived.

The Arrival and Departure of Adam and Eve at Dover

I

At the gate, expelled from the fable
of the East, the man's profile turned towards
the ullulating distraught woman.

And behind this couple now stumbling forward
— she half-bent over in her weeping —
the distant blitz-light of an angel.

II

So many thousands of centuries passed
and, in their innocence, new friends eased them
of the bdellium, the onyx stone
and the little gold acquired in Havilah.

So many more miles of thorns and thistles,
so many more winters howled away
before they came, at last, penniless,
to the alerted paparazzi at Dover.

The fuss! The fuss! The woman moaned on,
inconsolable, but the man seemed composed
until secular officials decreed
they faced no danger in their native country.

The Home Secretary (appealed to) said,
'At the end of the day' and 'God is merciful'.
Ceremonious duty done the two
'economic migrants' were repatriated.

On TV newsreels see them stepping from
a police van, discharged from this little world,
this scepter'd isle, this other Eden,
still in disgrace, coats over their heads.

Soho: Saturday Night

Always Cain, anonymous amidst the poor,
Abel dead in his eye, and over his damned sore
a khaki muffler, loiters, a fugitive in Soho,
enters The Golden Calf Club and hears Esau,

dishevelled and drunk, cursing kith and kin.
'A mess of pottage!' Esau strokes an unshaven chin
and strikes a marble table-top. Then hairy hands
fidget dolefully, raise up a glass of gin.

Outside, Joseph, dyspnoeic, regards a star
convexing over Dean street, coughs up a flower
from ruined lungs — rosy petals on his tongue —
recalls the Pit and wounds of many a colour.

Traffic lights change. With tapping white stick
a giant crosses the road between the frantic
taxis. A philistine pimp laughs. Dancing
in The Nude Show Delilah suddenly feels sick.

Ruth, too, the innocent, was gullibly led,
lay down half-clothed on a brassy railing bed
of Mr Boaz of Bayswater. Now, too late, weeps
antiseptic tears, wishes she were dead.

Who goes home? Nebuchadnezzar to the doss-
house where, all night, he'll turn and toss.
Lunchtime, in Soho Square, he munched the grass
and now he howls at strangers as they pass.

In Café Babylon, Daniel, interpreter of dreams,
listens to Belshazzar, a shy lad in his teens:
'A soiled finger moved across the lavatory wall.'

Growing up is not so easy as it seems.

Prophets, like tipsters, awaiting the Advent.
Beggar Job, under the flashing advertisement
for toothpaste, the spirochaete in his brain,
groans. Chalks a lurid picture on the pavement.

The Golden Calf closes. Who goes home? All
tourists to Nod, psalmists from their pub crawl;
they leave unshaved Soho to its dawn furnace
of affliction, its wormwood and its gall.

No Lazarus

At the time of the Resurrection
not one person rose up
from the cemeteries of London.
But, at Marylebone Road,
a procession of clothed dummies
streamed out of Madame Tussaud's,
arms raised, wild, shouting Hallelujah.

The Archbishop of Canterbury
and other official sources
denied a computer error.

Inscription on the Flyleaf of a Bible

(*For Larne*)

Doubting, read what this fabled history teaches,
how the firework, Imagination, reaches high
to dignify and sanctify.

You need not, granddaughter, be religious
to learn what Judges, Kings, Prophets, yield,
thought-lanterns for Life's darker field,
moral lies of piety and poetry.

You need not, granddaughter, hosanna heroes:
this wily shepherd, that bloodthirsty tough;
yet applaud the bulrush child
who, when offered gold, chose the coal.
Satisfied, the tyrant Pharaoh smiled,
did not see the pattern in the whole.

Forgive the triumphalism and the pride,
forego the curses and the ritual stuff.
You, older, I hope, will always side
with the enslaved and hunted,
deride the loud and lethal crowd
who vilify and simplify.

What is poetry but the first words
Adam, amazed, spoke to Eve?
On the first page of Genesis
hear the next to Nothing.
Later sound-effects, God off-stage, or theurgic stunts,
(water from a rock, a bush ablaze) might deceive
but bring ladders only to nerveless heaven.
Better to walk with Jephthah's luckless daughter

among real hills. And grieve.

Enjoy David's winging gifts to praise;
Solomon's rapturous serenade; also Job's
night-starred elegance of distress —
though such eloquence can bless,
indiscriminately, the last flags of the just
and the unjust on the barricade.

Read, granddaughter, these scandalous stories,
screaming Joseph in the pit of scorpions,
champion Goliath of course outclassed;
so many cubits of sorrow and delight,
so many visions of our ruffian Past.
They do not stale or fade
and may fortify and mollify.

Events Leading to the Conception of Solomon, The Wise Child

And David comforted Bathsheba his wife, and went into her, and lay with her; and she bore a son, and he called his name Solomon: and the Lord loved him.

I

Are the omina favourable?
Scribes know the King's spittle,
even the most honoured
like Seraiah the Canaanite,
and there are those, addicted,
who inhale
              the smoke of burning papyrus.

So is the date-wine sour, the lemon sweet?
Who can hear the sun's furnace?

The shadow of some great bird
              drifts indolently
across the ochres and umbers
of the afternoon hills
              that surround Jerusalem.
Their rising contours, their heat-refracting
              undulations.

The lizard is on the ledges,
the snake is in the crevices.

It is where Time lives.

Below, within the thermals of the Royal
              City,

past the cursing camel driver,

past the sweating woman carrying water
        in a goatskin,
past the leper peeping through
        the lateral slats
of his fly-mongering latrine
to the walls of the Palace itself,
the chanting King is at prayer.

        Aha, aha,
attend to my cry, O Lord
who makest beauty
to be consumed away like a moth;
purge me with hyssop and I
        shall be clean.
Wash me and I shall be whiter
        than the blossom.
Blot out my iniquities.

Not yet this prayer, not yet
        that psalm.
It is where a story begins.
Even the bedouin beside their black tents
have heard the desert wind's rumour.
They ask:
        Can papyrus grow
where there is no marsh?
They cry:
        Sopher yodea
to the Scribe with two tongues,
urge him to tend his kingdom
of impertinence.

II

When the naked lady stooped to bathe
   in the gushings of a spring,
the voyeur on the tower roof
   just happened to be the King.

She was summoned to the Palace
   where the King displayed his charms;
he stroked the harp's glissandos,
   sang her a couple of psalms.

Majestic sweet-talk in the Palace
   — he name-dropped Goliath and Saul —
till only one candle-flame flickered
   and two shadows moved close on the wall.

Of course she hankered for the Palace.
   Royal charisma switched her on.
Her husband snored at the Eastern Front,
   so first a kiss, then scruples gone.

Some say, 'Sweet victim in the Palace,'
   some say, 'Poor lady in his bed.'
But Bathsheba's teeth like milk were white,
   and her mouth like wine was red.

David, at breakfast, bit an apple.
   She, playful, giggling, seized his crown,
then the apple-flesh as usual
   after the bite turned brown.

III

In the kitchen, the gregarious, hovering flies
where the servants breakfast.
A peacock struts
        in its irradiance,
and is ignored.

On the stone floor and on the shelves
the lovely shapes of utensils,
great clay pots, many jugs of wine
        many horns of oil,
the food-vessels and the feast-boards.

On the long table, butter of kine, thin loaves,
bowls of olives and griddle-cakes,
wattled baskets of summer fruit,
flasks of asses' milk and jars of honey.

What a tumult of tongues,
        the maids and the men,
the hewers of wood,
the drawers of water,
        the narrow-skulled
        and the wide-faced.
What a momentary freedom prospers,
        a detour from routine,
a substitute for mild insurrection.

They ask:
    In his arras-hung chamber
    did the King smell of the sheepcote?
    On the ivory bench, did he seat her
        on cushions?
    Did she lie on the braided crimson couch,
    beneath her head pillows of goat hair?

Who saw him undo her raiments?
Who overheard Uriah's wife,
Bathsheba of the small voice,
     cry out?
Was it a woman made love to
or the nocturnal moan
      of the turtle dove?
Will the priest, Nathan, awaken
who, even in his sleep, mutters
      Abomination?

Now she who is beautiful to look upon
leaves furtively by a back door.
She will become a public secret.
She wears fresh garments of blue and purple,
the topaz of Ethiopia beneath her apparel.
But a wind gossips in the palm trees,
the anaphora of the wind
        in the fir-trees of Senir,
        in the cedars of Lebanon,
        in the oaks of Bashan.
It flaps the tents where Uriah, the Hittite,
is encamped with Joab's army
on the Eastern open fields.

Does purity of lust last one night only?
In the breakfasting kitchen, the peacock screams.

IV

The wind blows and the page turns over.
   Soon the King was reading a note.
Oh such excruciating Hebrew:
   'I've one in the bin,' she wrote.

114

Since scandal's bad for royal business
    the King must not father the child;
so he called Uriah from the front,
    shook his hand like a voter. Smiled.

Uriah had scorned the wind's whisper,
    raised his eyebrows in disbelief.
Still, here was the King praising his valour,
    here was the King granting him leave.

In uniform rough as a cat's tongue
    the soldier artlessly said,
'Hard are the stones on the Eastern Front,
    but, Sire, harder at home is my bed.'

Though flagons and goat-meat were offered
    the Hittite refused to go home.
He lingered outside the Palace gates,
    big eyes as dark as the tomb.

Silk merchants came and departed,
    they turned from Uriah appalled —
for the soldier sobbed in the stony heat,
    ignored his wife when she called;

sat down with his sacks, sat in the sun,
    sat under stars and would not quit,
scowled at the King accusingly
    till the King got fed up with it.

'Stubborn Uriah, what do you want?
    Land? Gold? Speak and I'll comply.'
Then two vultures creaked overhead
    to brighten the Hittite's eye.

'Death.' That's what he sought in the desert
    near some nameless stony track.
And there two vultures ate the soldier
    with a dagger in his back.

The widow was brought to the Palace,
    a Queen for the King-size bed,
and oh their teeth like milk were white,
    and their mouths like wine were red.

V

Should there be merriment at a funeral?
Stones of Jerusalem, where is your lament?
Should her face not have been leper-ashen?
Should she not have torn at her apparel
        bayed at the moon?
Is first young love
        always a malady?

When Uriah roared with the Captains of Joab,
        the swearing garrisons,
the dust leaping behind the chariots,
        the wagons, the wheels;
when his sword was unsheathed
amidst the uplifted trumpets
and the cacophony of donkeys;
when he was fierce as a close-up,
        huge with shield and helmet;
when his face was smeared with vermilion,
did she think of him less
        than a scarecrow in a field?

When she was more girl than woman
who built for her

116

a house of four pillars?
When his foot was sore
        did she not dip it in oil?
When his fever seemed perilous
        did she not boil the figs?

When the morning stars sang together,
face to face, they sang together.
At night when she shyly stooped
        did he not boldly soar?

When, at midnight, the owl screeched
        who comforted her?
When the unclothed satyr danced
        in moonlight
who raised a handkerchief to her wide eyes?

When the archers practiced
        in the green pastures
whose steady arm curled about her waist?

True love is not briefly displayed
like the noon glory of the fig marigold.

Return oh return
pigeons of memory to your homing land.

But the scent was only a guest
        in the orange tree.
The colours faded
        from the ardent flowers
not wishing to outstay their visit.

VI

The wind blows and the page turns over.
    To Bathsheba a babe was born.
Alas, the child would not feed by day,
    by night coughed like a thunderstorm.

'Let there be justice after sunset,'
    cried Nathan, the raging priest.
Once again he cursed the ailing child
    and the women's sobs increased.

So the skeletal baby sickened
    while the King by the cot-side prayed
and the insomniac mother stared
    at a crack in the wall afraid.

Nobody played the psaltery,
    nobody dared the gameboard.
The red heifer and doves were slaughtered.
    A bored soldier cleaned his stained sword.

Courtiers huddled in the courtyard,
    rampant their whisperings of malice.
The concubines strutted their blacks.
    The spider was in the Palace.

Soon a battery of doors in the Palace,
    soon a weird shout, 'The child is dead.'
Then Bathsheba's teeth like milk were white,
    and her eyes like wine were red.

Outside the theatre of the shrine
    David's penitent spirit soared
beyond the trapped stars. He wept. He danced
    the dance of death before the Lord.

That night the King climbed to her bedroom.
    Gently he coaxed the bereaved
and in their shared and naked suffering
    the wise child, love, was conceived.

CODA

Over the rocky dorsals of the hills
the pilgrim buses of April arrive,
one by one, into Jerusalem.

There was a jackal on the site
            of the Temple
before the Temple was built.

And stones. The stones only.

Are the omina favourable?
Will there be blood on the thorn bush?
Does smoke rising from the rubbish dump
            veer to the West or to the East?
So much daylight! So much dust!
This scribe is
            and is not
the Scribe who knew the King's spittle.

After the soldier alighted,
a black-bearded, invalid-faced man,
stern as Nathan, head covered,
followed by a fat woman, a tourist
wearing the same Phoenician purple
            as once Bathsheba did,
her jeweled wrist, for one moment,
a drizzle of electric.

But no bizarre crowned phantom
will sign the Register
       at the King David Hotel.

Like the lethargic darkness
of 3000 years ago,
once captive, cornered
within the narrow-windowed
       Temple of Solomon,
everything has vanished into the light.

Except the stones. The stones only.

There is a bazaar-loud haggling
       in the chiaroscuro
        of the alleyways,
tongue-gossip in the gravel walks,
even in the oven of the Squares,
a discontinuous, secret weeping
of a husband or wife, belittled and betrayed
behind the shut door of an unrecorded house.

There is a kissing of the stones,
a kneeling on the stones,
       psalmody and hymnody,
winged prayers swarming in the domed hives
of mosques, synagogues, churches,
ebullitions of harsh religion.

— For thou art my lamp, O Lord . . .
— In the name of God, Lord of the Worlds . . .
— Hear the voice of my supplications . . .
— And forgive us our trespasses . . .
— The Lord is my shepherd I shall not want . . .
— My fortress, my high tower, my deliverer . . .

— The Lord is my shepherd I shall not . . .
        . . . my buckler, my hiding place . . .
— I am poured out like water . . .
— The Lord is my shepherd . . .
        . . . and my bones are vexed . . .
— The Lord is . . .
            — Allah Akbar!
            — Sovereign of the Universe!
            — Our Father in Heaven!
            — Father of Mercies!
            — Shema Yisroael!

There is a tremendous hush in the hills
        above the hills
where the lizard is on the ledges,
where the snake is in the crevices,
after the shadow of an aeroplane
        has hurtled and leapt
below the hills and on to the hills
        that surround Jerusalem.

Notes

History

According to legend, a Chinese general defending a city long besieged by the Mongols climbed, late at night, on the battlements, knowing that in the morning he would have to surrender to the enemy encamped below. With utter sadness he played on his pipe a Mongolian melody. Such was the power of his music the Mongols became homesick and by dawn had departed!

Meurig Dafydd to His Mistress

The ruins of Beaupre (in Welsh Bewpyr), a once magnificent Tudor mansion, can be visited in the Vale of Glamorgan. There, after Christmas in 1603, a party was held at which a local bard, Meurig Dafydd, declaimed his praise-poem dedicated to the squire. Afterwards Meurig was asked if he had another copy of his poem. 'No by my fayth,' replied the bard, 'but I hope to take a copie of that which I delivered to you.' John Stradling, one of the guests, an English man of letters, reported how the bard's praise-poem was then delivered to the fire. A version of this incident is related in *The Taliesin Tradition* by Emyr Humphreys (Seren Books, 1989).

Ghosting for Mayakovsky

On the morning of 14 April 1930, the Soviet poet, Mayakovsky, shot himself. A fragment from an unfinished longer poem was included in his suicide note. A memorable version of this fragment, translated by Erik Korn, can be found in *Modern European Verse* (Vista Books, 1964). I have impudently 'ghosted' a later imagined draft of Mayakovsky's unfinished suicide poem, leaning on a few lines of Korn's translation.

Breakfast Together

The origin of this poem can be found in *Forbidden Games and Video Poems*, the poetry of Yang Mu and Lo Ch'ing (University of Washington Press, 1993). See Lo Ch'ing's 'Self-Sacrifice'.

Just One of Those Days, William

In the Introduction to *The Metamorphosis of Antoninus Liberalis* (Routledge, 1992) Francis Celoria relates how a crow was observed imitating the movements of seagulls at Middlesex Reservoir, 'despite an obvious inability to cope with a watery element'.

Lais was a celebrated whore of Corinth visited by princes, noblemen, orators and philosophers.

Agrius and Orius were the huge offspring of Polyphonte who had coupled with a bear.

Hylas was a river of Mysia where Hylas was drowned. Francis Celoria has written that Hylas was 'a lone waif, young and too pretty for his own good'.

On the Evening Road

The Caladrius bird was a white prophetic bird of medieval legend, supposed to visit the sick. If it looked at the patient, he or she would recover; if the bird looked away instead, the patient would die.

O Taste and See

The thirtysix just men, according to the Jewish legend of the Lamed-vaf, emerge in each generation to receive unto themselves the world's grief.

The Boasts of Hywel ab Owain Gwynedd

Hywel, who died in 1170, boasted in his poetry of the beauty of the landscape and the women of Merionethshire, his home county in northwest Wales. My poem, an imaginary one, is based on Hywel's 'Boast of Women' composed in the 12th century.

Lament of Heledd

Sections of a 9th century Welsh saga narrative have survived including one that refers to the destruction of Cynddylan's Hall (near Shrewsbury) by the English. All Cynddylan's family were killed with the exception of his sister, Heledd. For the first part of the present elegy I have imagined lost lines; the second part has been freely adapted from a revision of the original by the Dorset poet and linguist, William Barnes (1801-1886).

The Stonebreaker

The poem refers to a painting of that name by John Brett, an artist on the periphery of the Pre-Raphaelite circle. He and the painter J.W. Inchbold were both instructed, for a time, by John Ruskin in the art of landscape painting.

A Letter from Ogmore-by-Sea

Ogmore-by-Sea is a village on the coast of South Wales between Cardiff and Swansea. T. Carmi (1925-1997), a celebrated Israeli poet. Iolo Morganwg (1747-1826) — a gifted Welsh poet, antiquarian and forger, prone to exaggeration. Tusker Rock, one mile offshore from Ogmore, visible when the tide is out, has, in the past, sunk many an unwary ship.

In the Welsh National Museum

The artist, Josef Herman, was born in Warsaw and arrived in Britain in 1940.

For the idea of the Golem see Gershom Scholem's *On the Kabbalah and its Symbolism* (Schocken Books, New York 1969).

Jacob Grimm writes about the golem of late Kabbalistic legend in *Journal for Hermits* (1808): 'After saying certain prayers and observing certain fast days, the Polish Jews make the figure of a man from clay or mud and when they pronounce the miraculous Shemhamphoras (the name of God) over him, he must come to life. He cannot speak, but he understands fairly well what is said or commanded. They call him golem and use him as a servant to do all sorts of housework. But he must never leave the house. On his forehead is written *emeth* (truth); every day he gains weight and becomes somewhat larger and stronger . . . For fear of him, they therefore erase the first letter so that nothing remains but *meth* (he is dead), whereupon he collapses and turns to clay again.'

Domestic

The second section of the poem 'Domestic' is a variation of some lines in 'The Claim' by T. Carmi. See *Selected Poems*, T. Carmi and Dan Pagis, Penguin Modern Poets, 1976.

Last Lunch

David Wright (1920-1994) was a South African poet who spent most of his life in England. W.S. (Jock) Graham (1918-1986), Thomas Blackburn (1916-1979), Stevie Smith (1902-1971).